The Path To Authentic Power

How To Make The Changes
That Change Everything

by Joe Stumpf

The Path To Authentic Power -How To Make The Changes
That Change Everything

.

Published by By Referral Only, Inc. 2035 Corte Del Nogal, Suite
200 Carlsbad, CA 92011 www.byreferralonly.com

Dedicated to my Inner Circle because you seek
authentic power in all you do!

Inroduction

As you may know or not know, I've been coaching for over a quarter of a century. With over a thousand one-on-one sessions, I've discovered that most people want *circumstances* to change; but they don't want to *personally* change all that much.

Very few people have the courage to change beliefs and change habits.

I like to say it this way: Everyone wants to be skinny, happy, and rich, but only a few have the courage to change the habits that make them unhealthy, miserable, and broke.

I know I want to change when the economy is better.

I know I want to change when my company is stronger.

I know I want to change when the stock market is better.

Those are all *circumstances.* What many people want to do is change when *circumstances* change versus *change their own habits and their own beliefs.*

The question I've been examining for 30 years is why do we struggle with change, and what can we do to change the things that will change everything?

Most people would like to be more authentic. Most people want to be more inspired. Most people want to be a higher version of themselves.

How many people are really *willing* to make the *changes* in your *habits* that are *needed* to be truly more authentic?

Change Is About Stripping The Mask Away

My hope is that by the time your done reading this, you will have a deeper understanding of how *enormous* the personal implications are when you say, "I want to change."

When you say, "I want to change," what you're really talking about is your *habits*. The habits that are conditioned in your childhood.

Even more ingrained are the habits that come from the deep, evolutionary, primitive past.

You know from my books that the most primitive habit is to survive. It's to stay safe. It's to be secure. The habit of creating a safe and secure, fully comfortable life that limits risks helps us hide our authentic power behind a mask called "play it safe."

Yet, it's true that your most important personal growth occurs *outside* your safe comfort zone. We grow personally when we step up and we take intelligent, healthy, risks.

Actually, you know in your own experience that the *real* juice in life is when you take off the "play it safe" mask and you allow yourself to be energized by the challenge.

But many times, have you caught yourself wanting and hoping for an easier, softer way or simply allowing security and circumstances to determine your challenges versus really seeking your security?

I mean, truly seeking your security in playing a bigger game and making your life all about stripping the mask away and truly revealing your authentic power?

Imagine living a life that its purpose is to live authentically every moment.

Imagine that. Imagine waking up and your purpose is to live a life authentically every moment.

What kind of power would that take?

I would call it *authentic power.* Authentic power is something that no one can give you. No one can make it happen for you. You must do the work to bring it out of you.

You can hang around people who demand authenticity, but they can't do it for you because authentic power is when you are guided by your *own* awareness, your *own* mindfulness, your *own* intentions, and that you consciously choose – with compassion, and empathy, and wisdom – to access your authentic power.

My hero's journey into this world of personal growth has been about finding – and changing – the parts of my personality that do not intend for me to be authentically powerful.

How many of you can recognize there are parts of your personality right now that do not intend for you to be authentically powerful?

How We Give Away Our Power

What I've discovered through years of reflection and different ways of gathering insight is how the *habit* of playing it safe so I feel secure is one of the ways I give my power away.

I give my power to people; I give my power to circumstances, hoping that they will shape my destiny and they will shape the direction of my life.

How many times have you given up your power in hopes that *others* will help shape and guide your destiny?

In the past, I've exhausted myself rearranging and controlling the external world to try to satisfy what I would call my insatiable hunger for approval, for appreciation, for acknowledgement, that gives me the *illusion* of feeling secure and significant.

Like many of you, I grew up in an environment where I was addicted to what others thought about me. For a long time, what *others* thought about me would determine what *I* thought about me.

Early in my childhood, what got woven into the fabric of my life was this habit of giving my power away to external sources in an attempt to feel more secure on the inside.

I wonder if you could relate to that in any way. But we both know that that's pretty futile. It's like having a hole in your bucket. No matter how much you put in, it's never enough.

It's taken me hundreds of hours, maybe thousands of hours, of self-reflection and exploration and really deep inner work to replace this habit with authentic power.

The 10 Keys To Authentic Power

As your coach, I know that even some of the most confident, candid, and seemingly empowered people – that appear to have it all – still feel, at their core, insecure.

The insecurity gets masked in clever ways.

It takes courage and trust to go within and find authentic power. But once you do, you start living a life of true, unconditional love and deep connection, and a lasting peace of mind.

Here are the 10 keys to authentic power and how to make the changes that change everything.

I know these 10 keys will open for you an entirely new way of being that is counter-intuitive to your instinctual, primitive way because I have focused on them, and I continue to focusing on these 10 keys each day that allow me to successfully connect to my authentic power and help me let go of that instinctual, primitive habit that keep me stuck.

What I want for you more than anything, is for you to live each day in the highest version of yourself, which is the part of you that is fully unrestricted and has complete access to authentic power.

#1 Learn From Your Fear In Insecurity

I know that behind most of my reactions is insecurity and fear. Behind my anger is fear and insecurity. Behind my guilt is fear and insecurity. Behind my apathy is fear and insecurity. Behind my shame is fear and insecurity. Just about any reaction that I have in life – behind it is fear and insecurity.

What I'm learning is to use my fear and insecurity *as a teacher.* I love that thought. I love the thought that fear and insecurity are teachers; they're like workshop leaders. Most recently, fear and insecurity are teaching me how to surrender and let go.

Play with me on this little exercise for just a minute; have some fun with this. Wherever you are right now, would you please raise your right hand if you have ever gotten into a situation where you felt fear about something or someone and you could not control that something or someone?

Would you raise your right hand if that's ever happened to you? Now keep your right hand up in the air. Now raise your left hand if you've ever witnessed a friend, a family member, or a client get fearful over something they had no control over. Now with both hands in the air, say to yourself out loud, "I surrender." "I surrender."

The word *surrender* is often interpreted as giving up, almost as a weakness or as admitting defeat. Although this is one way that we can use the word, we're going to use it in a very empowering and very different way.

Today, *surrender* means letting go of the belief and the habit that no longer represents the version of you that you want to create.

Surrender does not diminish our power; it enhances it. For example, during a Crossfit workout that I we were doing a dead lift evolution. We were told to do 90% of our maximum weight 15 times. My coach, said to me, "Joe, you're now ready for 295 pounds." I didn't say a word, but I did think, "I don't want to get hurt."

Coach looked at me as if he read my mind.

He said, "Number one: Lift with your legs.

Number two: Open your hips.

Number three: Keep your butt tight.

Number four: Breathe in when you pick up the weights.

Number five: Breathe out when you put it down. And Joe, you will be safe."

What I learned in that moment was the difference between an amateur – that was me – and the pro.

The amateur's first habit of thought is *focusing on what they don't want.*

The pro...their first habit of thought is *what are the steps to do it right.*

Amateurs go into fear and insecurity and get stuck. It's primitive. It's natural.

Pros have an awareness that goes to the solution and finds the steps to move forward.

"I Surrender"

What all fear does is test your resolve.

Fear asks of you, "What do you believe?"

Fear asks, "What are your habits?"

Fear asks you, "What decisions have you made and what is really important to you?"

As I move through my workout, I'm saying to myself, I'm saying to myself, "Joe, surrender. Joe, let go and open to the highest version of who you really are. Be open, Joe. Be open for coaching. Fear is asking for instruction. Insecurity is asking for leadership. Insecurity and fear is asking to trust that I will find the safest, best way to achieve whatever is asked of me.

Surrender, Joe. Let go. Play big. Surrender, Joe. Let go. Be a team player. Surrender, Joe. Let go. Move faster. Surrender, Joe. Create your destiny. Surrender, Joe. Complete what you start."

As I discover what I'm letting go of, as I discover that I'm surrendering, that 295 pounds is easier to lift without fear and insecurity hanging all over it.

What is going on in your life right now?

Right now, what's going on in your life that is asking you to surrender to, that is asking you to let go of?

What is asking you to play bigger?

What is asking you right now to be a better team player?

What's asking you just to move faster?

What's asking you to finish what you start?

What's asking you to surrender and let go?

Experience shows that you'll find your authentic power when you choose your words to match what you want. That's why it's so important that you do the work to create a clear intention for what you want.

Find the words that describe your beliefs. Find the words that describe your new habits. Find the words that describe the decisions that you've made and repeat them over and over and over until you surrender to them.

#2 Listen To What Your Body Is Saying, But Let Your Mind Direct Your Body

Right now, can you listen with your body? When I say the word "surrender" or you say the word "surrender," where do you feel it in your body? Listen to what I'm saying with your body. Listen right now with your body. Feel it in your body. What's going on right now in your body?

Coach Thomas Leonard taught me that the body never lies. Listening to your body brings you in direct awareness with your authentic power. It's when your authentic power is most alive. Right now, move from your head to your body. Maybe you have to take your hand and just put it on your chest and listen to your body. What do you feel? Where do you feel it? Is surrendering in your gut? Is surrendering in your throat? Is surrendering in your chest? Where do you feel it right now? When you're called to show up in a way that you've never shown up before, where do you feel it? What does it feel like? Right now, that's your authentic power just busting out, just wanting to be released.

Feel **Where The Answer Is**

When I ask you, "What do you want to most create in your life?"

Get quiet. Right now, get quiet. What do you most want to create in your life?

Go inside. Close your eyes and ask your body "What do you want to create in your life right now?"

Before you put words to it, *feel* where the answer is. Is it in your head? Is it in your shoulders? Is it in your chest? Is it in your stomach? Find where it lives in your body and stay with it.

Stay with me on this. Stay here with me because this is how you find your authentic power.

The other day, a good friend of mine asked me to close my eyes and then asked me why I did the SealFit Kokoro experience.

She thought this was just a really extraordinary experience. She goes, "Why did you do it?"

Then she said, "Find the answer inside your body." Then she said, "Put your hand on the part of your body where the answer is coming from." I felt this energy in my throat. She said, "What does the throat want to give voice to?" I said, "I wanted to find my voice. My experience that is unique to me." She said, "What is important about finding that voice? Put your hand on your body where the answer is."

I felt a turn in my stomach. I put on my hand on my gut and she said, "What voice did SealFit want to give birth to?" That thought, "SealFit is gave birth to a voice that has been stuck or trapped inside me that has gone largely unexpressed," cracked me wide open. I could feel a rush of emotion and tears just flow through my body.

Then the words I spoke were, "I gave birth to *my* authentic voice. I wanted to experience *my* journey into believing in me, and *my* message that is truly, authentically mine." My symbol for what is blocking me is a voice that is trapped inside my gut wanting to be birthed as my unique, authentic power; it's my symbol. I wanted to dissolve this symbol of the trapped voice. I've chose my SealFit challenge to be the symbol – or the metaphor – that matches the importance of the birthing of the voice.

Ask yourself, "What do you want?" And find the answer inside your body. Then create a symbol – or a metaphor – that your body is *holding* which will be *dissolved* – or birthed – through the symbol or the metaphor that matches in importance.

What event have you chosen as your metaphor that will give voice to a more authentic power within you?

Joseph Campbell says it well in just a few words. He says, "The goal of the hero's journey is to find yourself." So key number two: Listen carefully to what your voice is saying *inside your body*.

What is it saying?

#3 Your Authentic Power Is To Fully Feel The Emotions That Your Thoughts Are Creating

I've noticed when I'm judging.

I notice when I'm over-analyzing.

Right now are you over-analyzing or are you judging?

Notice when you're comparing yourself to others. I notice when I'm comparing myself to others. I notice when I'm over-planning; I notice that. I can see those thoughts and feel those thoughts. I also focus when I'm grateful and when I'm appreciative. I notice what it feels like to be open and vulnerable.

Personal growth – or personal development – is practicing daily, and developing your awareness of being *mindful* of what thoughts create what emotions.

We are what we think. I love what the Buddha says: "All that we are arises with our thoughts. With our thoughts, we make our world."

Thoughts and emotions happen as a result of your interaction with the world based on your perception of past experiences. It's the way the mind works. How you and I perceive the world helps us form our thoughts that become our reactions and our behaviors, both unconsciously and consciously.

If we perceive the world as unfriendly, it helps us form thoughts that become protective and harsh or quick to defend.

We may not even be conscious until someone lovingly points it out and helps us into new awareness. After all, your thoughts create your feelings. Your thoughts create your emotions. Your thoughts create your behavior. What you attract into your life is a result of what you've been thinking about for a long time. Just look around you. It's evidence of what you're thinking.

The good part is this. This is the good news and I love this thought: **Emotions are the fuel for creation.** We need emotion. Everything you dwell upon in your mind and your heart, everything that you believe in is drawn into physical manifestation.

The more emotion you put behind that, the faster it is manifested. Thank goodness for feelings that create emotions.

Feelings and emotions are what *ignite* your desire and create what you want. Right now, just ask yourself – one low/1 ten high – how happy do you feel?

Right now, how happy do you feel? Pick a happier thought. Notice that if you dare to feel really good, make a thought that's even happier. If you really want to feel great, make a list of 50 things that you're grateful for *only* if you really, really, really want to put some strong emotion behind your creation. I love that thought. Gratitude is the fuel for creation because it's such a *high* level of octane emotion. Energy in motion.

#4 Being Your Most Authentic Self Is Being Honest About Your Intentions

I've noticed that when my intention is to be *right* versus to be *happy,* I start seeking your approval.

I notice when my intention is for your admiration and your acknowledgment; I can notice that. I can notice that when I'm trying to convince you as my intention.

I also can notice when I'm cooperating. I also notice when my intention is to truly share and really serve life.

What Is My Intention Behind My Behavior?

I wonder, I really wonder, what is your level of awareness around your intentions? Right now, as you learn about yourself and you how you react in life, ask yourself, "What is my intention?" You know that the most important question you can ever ask is, "What is my intention behind my behavior?"

When you're helping a person access their truth what you're really accessing is their most authentic intention.

The truth is their authentic intention.

Are you aware of your truth in every interaction?

For example:

1. What's important about being in your authentic power to you?

What's important about (answer #1) to you?

_____

What's important about (answer #2) to you?

_____

What's important about (answer #3) to you?

_____

What's important about (answer #4) to you?

_____

What's important about (answer #5) to you?

_____

What's important about (answer #6) to you?

_____

What's important about (answer #7) to you?

_____

As you answer it 7 times and get closer to your truth.

I love what Doctor David Hawkins says: "There is nothing false. There's just more truth." The more truth you tell, the more connected you are to your intention.

Your authentic power can be found in your true intention.

The question I'm always asking is, "What's my intention here?" It releases authentic power.

#5 Be Willing To Take Full Responsibility For Everything

Now the key is be willing to take full responsibility for everything: full responsibility for my feelings, full responsibility for my experience, full responsibility for my actions. No blaming going on here.

When it comes to taking responsibility, I either do or I don't. There is no in-between here. Everything that is happening in my life, everything that his happening in my business right now, I'm 100% responsible for.

Creating authentic power means becoming the true authority in my life and in my business. Now, who knows more about you – than you? Who knows more about me – than me? Who knows more about your business – than you? Who knows more about my business – than me?

Who knows more about how *you* feel than you?

Who knows more about what you're experiencing than you?

Who cares more about your aspirations than *you*?

When you get advice or when you get input, you're the ultimate authority. You're responsible. When you get some advice or when you get some insight, *you* are responsible whether you take it or not.

When you hear something; when you listen with all your senses. And if someone gives you an insight and they say,

"This is what I would recommend that you do," you listen fully because you're responsible.

If you do it and it doesn't work, you're responsible because you did it and it didn't work. You're responsible if the outcome is working or it's not working. It's not them. It's not me.

***You're* responsible. That's exciting.**

I love that thought. What I love to do is when I get advice, and I seek advice from others. But when I get advice or insight or input, I always ask myself, "Is what I'm receiving right now really worth remembering?"

Does it resonate? I mean right now? Is this even worth remembering? Does it even resonate with you?

If it does resonate, at what level does it resonate? Does it resonate on a level that's really worth remembering? If it doesn't resonate in my body, if it doesn't resonate in my mind, if it doesn't resonate for me, and if doesn't vibrate for me, if it doesn't feel right for me, I let it go.

If it doesn't resonate in my gut, if I don't feel it, I let it go. If it doesn't resonate, I just say, "You know what? That's not even worth remembering," and I let it go.

So if somebody criticizes me and they give me feedback and I go, "Does it even resonate?

Do I even feel it?" If it doesn't resonate, "That's not worth remembering."

However, if somebody says something to me and it resonates and I feel it in my gut, I know that it resonates.

Something must be true and I take responsibility for it.

Taking responsibility means everything happens for a reason. Sometimes your awareness is not developed enough to understand why it's happening.

All that really counts is your *willingness* to take responsibility for everything. That's why you're going to find your most authentic power:

Because you're willing to take responsibility for everything.

#6 Stay In Integrity At All Costs, Which Means I Speak And Tell The Truth In A Responsible Way Even When It Frightens You

When I don't want to talk, when my body wants to shut down, when I feel it in my gut closing down, I know that's when it is most important to speak. I call that moment when I want to shut down "the wall."

When the wall goes up, I'm out of integrity. I'm no longer authentic.

Integrity is telling the truth about what is going on in a responsible way. When you find that voice, you have found your authentic power.

I would love you to write a Letter From The Heart about your awareness when your wall rises and how you bring awareness to it, and how you access your integrity when your wall rises and you speak directly to it at all costs.

That's where your authentic voice lives.

I wrote a Letter From The Heart sharing my wall experience that I had in Rome, Italy. On the next page is my letter from the heart.

Tell The Truth And
"The Wall" Disappears

As soon as you make a commitment to do something big, the world will conspire to help you if you take action immediately.

A week after my return from Italy I sent an email to my new friend Peggy Markel telling her how much I missed Italy and the nurturing experience. I sent her a copy of my Letter From The Heart from the October *On Your Team* newsletter. Within 20 minutes Peggy responded by saying, "The only solution is to return as soon as possible." Then she invited me to stay at her home for 10 days if I could arrive the following week.

When I got the invitation my heart pounded. I could feel the immediate pull as if the benevolent universe was saying, "You asked for it – now here it is." At that moment I didn't know, but I heard a voice say, "The answer to 'how?' is 'yes.'" Today I know what the voice was leading me toward.

I granted myself instant permission to go into a deeper relationship with a person I hardly knew. I had no idea what was going to happen, but I knew that nothing significant happens inside my current comfort zone so I must challenge myself. So off I went, 17 hours of traveling from San Diego to New York to Paris to Florence.

When I arrived I jumped in a cab and traveled to Peggy's little apartment a block behind the Palazzo Vecchio. Peggy welcomed me into her fifth-floor apartment. My bedroom was a small 12' x 12' room on the roof of the building. I called it the "Pigeonhole." It had a perfect view of La Torre d'Arnolfo (the tower) built in 1299, the place where Michelangelo, Leonardo Da Vinci, Galileo, and Dante explored the questions that shaped civilization.

I breathed deeply and meditated on accessing their curiosity, their intensity, and their thirst for creating a new possibility for my life.

I felt like a sculpture was inside me, but it was hidden in a block of hardened consumerism nestled inside a world of narcissism.

As I looked out over the terracotta tiled roofs I felt the power of truth. I knew that I would discover inside me my *David,* but I didn't know that *I* was an answer to Peggy's prayer. That powers greater than us collaborated to bring us together to sculpt our souls.

We took out our chisels and mallets in the form of endless dialogue and profound, insightful conversation, and we channeled our new awareness.

Peggy is a very accomplished entrepreneur. She owns a company called Peggy Markel's Culinary Adventures (www.peggymarkel.com). For the last 17 years she's run Culinary Adventures in Morocco, Sicily, Florence, and the Amalfi Coast.

They are experiences revolving around three key life aspects:

Time. Learning how to invest uninterrupted chunks of time in cultures that offer a depth of grit and grace not readily available in the New World.

Food. Learning how food is for nurturing the absolute essence of your soul. Her approach to cooking is straightforward. It requires that type of attention on quality of ingredients, simple preparations, and joy of cooking for and with others...a taste that leaves your belly so full of love, that it begs for more.

Conversation. Learning how to have the type of conversa- tion that is intimate and authentic. Speaking in a way that opens you to profound new ways of being with each other.

Peggy's philosophy is, *Time, plus great food prepared with love, plus people coming together to share themselves, create a nurturing environment.* Peggy taught me that these three therapies – time, food, and conversation – heal us by nurturing us.

Within a few days my healing began, and I could feel the crack in my marble as I got glimmers of possibilities of living a life fully expressed. As I got to know Peggy I realized she was unlike any goddess I had encountered. She brilliantly met me where I was, and she felt equally met by me.

Together we chiseled away, moment by moment, episode by episode. As the old marble fell chunk by chunk, each clank of the chisel, each whack of the mallet revealed more. It really was like what Michelangelo said: *"David* was in there. All I had to do take away the excess marble."

On October 28 Peggy invited me to Rome to visit the seed of civilization. We stayed at the Portrait Suites, a stone's throw from the Spanish Steps. We walked the streets of Rome, laughing and playing, taking photos, uploading them onto Facebook – everything was *perfecto*.

Now here is where my story turns inward.

I want to give you a wonderful gift that was given to me.

Before I give this to you – you must know I have invested a majority of my adult life getting over the first 10 years of my childhood. I have been sober for 24 years, in therapy for 17 years, I have read literally thousands of books on personal development, I have done every workshop I can find that offered specific ways to open to my more authentic self.

So what I want you to know is that what happened on October 29 at 10am is the single most profound insight or shift I have ever had – but it has taken all my work to get to this place that I can say this.

We were at a five-star resort – we had had the mostmemorable, fun, creative, inventive, insightful, conscious connection that I can remember. We met each other at a level of intensity that was remarkable. All my signals were, "This is a woman I can fully open my heart to."

But...I was feeling something else. It was as if a wall was being constructed to shut her out. It felt like a team of 20 concrete guys rushing in to build this barrier that would shut out anything good.

I was witnessing the construction of "The Wall."

It was like I was on my deathbed, and all my regrets flashed in front of me. I could see that every intimate relationship I had ever been in had gotten to this moment, and then "The Wall" would be constructed.

However, this time I said, "Peggy, right now, right now I can feel it. 'The Wall' is being built right now – to close you out right now." I said, "I can feel myself pushing you away and I am about to call it something else."

Then the miracle occurred.

As soon as I named it "The Wall," *it* disappeared – not me.

Peggy knew what was happening and she felt it. In that moment she had the consciousness to know the magnitude of what I was doing, and she supported it fully as she watched it happen right before her eyes.

"The Wall" was exposed because I told the truth.

The truth knocked "The Wall" down.

I don't know where the relationship with Peggy and I will go. I do know I want to be in relationship with her, with no walls.

I do know my relationship with Peggy is built on trust because I know how to tell the truth.

And I also know "The Wall" doesn't.

Your Lighthouse Leader, Joe

#7 Say What Is Difficult To Say

Now unless you pull the bow, the arrow of thought cannot fly. I love that. I don't know who said that, but I love that thought. Unless you pull the bow, the arrow of thought cannot fly.

David Whyte I think he's the greatest living poet. He has this poem called, "Start Close In." You've heard me recite this.

It goes, "Start close in.

Don't take the second step or the third step.

Start with the first step.

The step you don't want to take.

Start close in.

Don't take the second step or the third step.

Start with the first.

The step you don't want to take.

The step that requires the most courage.

The step that will make you more human. More fully present."

What step will make you more real?

What do you have to say that will make you more real?

Not what step will make you more *comfortable,* but what step will make you *more real?*

I love the thought that life is not about being comfortable. Certainly an *authentic* life is not about being comfortable. An *authentic* life is about unfolding your authentic power.

You access your authentic power when you say what is difficult to say. What you have to say that may be difficult to say is where your authentic power lives.

#8 Releasing Any Distance You Feel From Anyone

"Dynamic Projection"

What I don't like in others is really what I don't like in myself. I'd like to thank Carl Jung for that thought. Carl Jung, a great therapist, said, "What you do not want to see in yourself, you project onto the world and see outside you." Carl called it "dynamic projection" and that's a tough one.

I know it's a tough one for me. It's a tough one for a guy like me who automatically loves to judge others.

This has been really a critical area on my path of authentic power.

For example, when I'm in a group of people, either I must have the willingness to walk up to someone in the room, or on a phone call, and say, "Hey, listen. I'm feeling some distance from you and there must be a part of me that I don't like that I see in you, and I want to clear that because this is where my authentic power is."

I gotta tell you, I've done that many, many times. That's the power of being part of a group of people who are all on the path to having a soulful significance where you make a difference authentically.

Extraordinary things can happen when you open yourself to a constant, fresh perspective with individual people in an authentic relationship. I can tell story after story after story of people who have come to me and have told me something that was creating distance between me and them. As soon as they shared with me that it was a projection that they had, it disappeared and they found their voice.

I invite you to do the same thing. When *you* are feeling distance, ask yourself what is it in that person that reminds me of the part of me that I'm not connected to? That if I could close the gap between myself and that person, I might close the gap between that part of me and the most authentic part of me? That takes enormous courage to find that power. But when you find it, you find a voice that is expressed in the world like no other.

#9 Be Present

Focus on opening yourself to being present while others are speaking.

Let me say that again. Focus on *opening* yourself to being present while others are speaking. I open myself to focus on being fully present while others are speaking.

This is not a communication trick or a technique. This is how you access your authentic power, by deeply listening to the *words* but more importantly, the *feelings* behind the words.

One of my coaches has helped me listen better when she taught me to *patiently*, and lovingly, and respectfully listen with respect, even when the other person is saying something that is complete nonsense. She calls it "with a curious heart." Open yourself to being present.

Open yourself to being present every time someone speaks. Listen with a curious heart. That's really worth practicing today, asking yourself, "Am I listening right now with a truly curious heart?

Am I present right now?" You'll find your authentic power lies in that moment.

#10 Non-Attached From The Outcome

I didn't say be *detached* from the outcome; I said be *non-attached* from the outcome.

Now, in business, I want to make as much money as possible. I want you to make as much money as possible. I want everyone to make as much money as possible. I want you to create enormous financial abundance for yourself. I want enormous wealth for myself. I want enormous financial abundance for my loved ones. I want extraordinary freedom.

I want choices. I want opportunity. I want to leave an incredible financial legacy. I want you to do the same.

I want to be aligned with my highest financial purpose. I want *you* to be aligned with your highest financial purpose.

I know that's what you want for yourself.

I know that's what you want for me.

You want financial security.

You want financial freedom.

I want financial security.

I want financial freedom.

You want so much money that you can make any choice that you want. You want to create opportunity for everyone that you love.

You want to leave an extraordinary financial legacy. You want to be financially aligned with the highest possible purpose on the planet.

Of course, we all want that. The best thing you could do for the poor is *not* be one of them. Abundance is a good thing because it's a reflection of what the market says has value.

You can *also* access your power, your authentic power, to create your abundance.

See, you could also access your manipulative power and control markets and control people and make lots of money. We've seen how people have done that in the past. It's temporary. It's manipulative. It's not authentic. You can see the old economy was based on manipulation, and control, and power, but not *authentic* power.

Authentic Power For The Authentic Economy

What I like to imagine is we're moving into an entirely new economy – it's the *authentic* economy. It's where you *have* to be authentic. You *have* to have authentic power.

The level of awareness and consciousness, right now, on the planet is at an all-time high. We're waking up. How are we waking up, because it's in complete chaos right now? It's in complete breakdown right now. Wherever there is a breakdown, there is an enormous, extraordinary opportunity for breakthrough.

The shift right now is from an unconscious economy to a conscious economy; from an unauthentic relationship with money to an authentic relationship with money; from power, control and manipulation to true, authentic power.

The more authentic place that you come from, the more authentic the place that you give, the more authentic you receive.

The more you detach from your control and manipulation, the more you find joy in every moment.

Authentic power comes when you let go of the narrative, all that mind chatter, all that stuff that's chattering away in your mind: "What will those people think of me? They'll think I'm weak in this area. What will they think? What will they think? They'll think that I'm this..."

That little whiny, chattery voice that doesn't get enough attention. You let go of that *mind* chatter and you directly experience yourself as willing to give your very best and receive what you need right now.

I love that thought a guy named Glass said. He said something very powerful. He says, "Is it better to give than receive?" And he said, "Neither. We give and we receive because giving is inhaling and receiving is exhaling.

You just don't do one or the other. You do them both." When you really let go and you bring out into the world the very highest, most authentic voice, your true power – you give.

In return, you receive.

And your willingness to receive is in direct relationship to your willingness to give.

But it is give and receive, your ability to authentically tell people where you can really help them.

Where can you really *help* them, not *impress* them, but truly *help* them is in direct relationship to your ability to completely expose yourself.

This is where I need my help. This is where you need help. Better yet, this is the area that I experience you being afraid of or this is the area that I'm afraid of.

This is the area that frightens me most. This is the area that I'm experiencing that frightens you most. This is the area that I notice you're avoiding in your life. This is the area that I'm avoiding in my life. That is the authentic voice. That is the new economy. The economy is helping people tell the truth and only helping people tell the truth that *you* have come into awareness with.

This was written by a By Referral Only member Drake Smith.

"I Need To Share My Vulnerability"

My expereince of being a member of the By Referral Only community has been eye-opening for me.

Over the past two weeks, I've been given the opportunity to reflect on life, not just in terms of my professional career but also my personal relationships with those closest to me.

"I've had to face some hard truths, but I know I will come

out of this process a better person. I've also had to deal with the fact that my actions and my attitude have severely limited my potential.

But through this experience, I've gained new strength, focus, and perspective. To my mentors, Joe and Dan," referring to Dan Paris, "I thank you for your pearls of wisdom.

I thank you for wanting more for me than I want for myself, and sharing your joy and your love. Because of you, I will have my most connected year ever.

"To the members my By Referral Only Do Group, I also thank you. I thank you for showing up.

Thank you for sharing your thoughts and your experiences with me and others in the group.

One of the dominating thoughts that has been flashing through my mind over the past two weeks is 'strength in numbers'.

While I'm fighting off the vulnerability demons every day, I'm comforted in the fact that I am on the right path, surrounded by my team members in the By Referral Only Community.

"I had to write this for a couple of reasons.

Number one, I needed to stop holding back. I needed to tell my truth which is that I've neglected those I care about far too long. I've insulated myself in this too many years of enrichment by not building relationships.

The great news is I'm now free, and I'm free to *share* joy and love and *receive* joy and love.

The second reason for this post is to let you know that I am here and prepared to give my thoughts and ideas as much as I receive. I need to share my vulnerability"

That's my new economy. "I need to share my vulnerability."

As You Read Drake's Letter; You Can Hear Him Getting Back His Power

He has found his authentic voice.

He is learning from his fear and insecurity.

He is learning to turn inward for answers.

He is learning to *master his* awareness of his thoughts.

He is learning to check his intentions moment by moment.

He is learning to take full responsibility for everything.

He is learning to make integrity his core value.

He is learning to do and say what is most difficult.

He is learning to release his distance from everyone and use that as a *model* in life to remove distance from everyone.

He is learning to be present when others speak.

He is learning non-attachment from the outcome and be fully invested in abundance by giving and receiving.

This is how you create your authentic power.

About Joe Stumpf

Joe Stumpf has been in and around the real estate coaching and training business since 1977.

In 1981, he started his training and coaching company, which has grown to be one of the largest coaching companies in North America.

Joe Stumpf has a subscription-based company with over 5,000 clients, the purpose of which is to teach the principles, provide the tools and systems, to be highly profitable and at the same time serve others with the heart of a "Super Servant".

Joe Stumpf invests most of his time and energy in creating, writing, and video/audio recording, while his leadership team runs his company's day-to-day operations.

His work has been a wonderful vehicle to express his creativity, as through it he gets to live a life fully expressed as a model of possibility.

It is the perfect forum for him to discover and allow his most authentic self to be publicly shared.

In all of Joe Stumpf's work his intention is to create the next version of himself, one which is more aligned with his soul-purpose.

He has gained a sense of mastery on the goal line while maintaining a sense of sacred purpose.

Reading, writing, teaching, and coaching is woven into his fabric.

He possesses a beautiful coaching gift of being able to channel insight and awareness to people when they seek clarity and direction in business and life.

He helps people in profound ways so they can experience the shifts they desire as a result of crossing his path.

He views this as his life's purpose.

You're welcome to take a closer look at Joe's work at MyByreferralOnly.com or you can write to Joe at JoeStumpf@gmail.com.

32856079R00027

Made in the USA
Charleston, SC
27 August 2014